Lifelines:
Wrestling the Word, Gathering Up Grace

Carla A. Grosch-Miller

CANTERBURY
PRESS
Norwich

© Carla A. Grosch-Miller 2020

First published in 2020 by the Canterbury Press Norwich
Editorial office
3rd Floor, Invicta House
108–114 Golden Lane
London EC1Y 0TG, UK
www.canterburypress.co.uk

Canterbury Press is an imprint of Hymns Ancient & Modern Ltd
(a registered charity)

Ancient
&Modern

Hymns Ancient & Modern® is a registered trademark of
Hymns Ancient & Modern Ltd
13A Hellesdon Park Road, Norwich,
Norfolk NR6 5DR, UK

All rights reserved. No part of this publication may be reproduced,
stored in a retrieval system, or transmitted,
in any form or by any means, electronic, mechanical,
photocopying or otherwise, without the prior permission of
the publisher, Canterbury Press.

The Author has asserted her right under the Copyright, Designs and
Patents Act 1988 to be identified as the Author of this Work

British Library Cataloguing in Publication data

A catalogue record for this book is available
from the British Library

978 1 78622 234 3

Typeset by Regent Typesetting
Printed and bound in Great Britain by
CPI Group (UK) Ltd

For David
whose steadiness keeps me standing
and whose encouragement enables me to soar

Contents

To the Reader	x
Genesis	xiv

Part 1 Wrestling the Word — 1

Lectionary Poems

Advent — 2
The Waiting	2
The Tender Shoot	3
The Call to Repent	4
Leaping	5
The Joseph Cycle	6
Meditation on Rembrandt's *The Holy Family by Night*	9
Expectant	9

Christmas — 10
Christmas Eve	10
Christmas Morn	11
The Slaughter of Innocence	11
Song of a Mother	12

Epiphany — 13
Star of Wisdom	13
Baptism of Jesus	13
The Tree	14
The Call	15
Make Peace	16
Becoming	17

In the Footsteps of Elijah	18
Holy	19
The Radiance!	20

Lent
Wild Beasts	21
For the Leader (Nicodemus)	22
Sarah Speaks	23
Temptation	24
Ode to Moses' Mum	25
There is a time	26
Hidden Depths	27
Dying to life	28
Passion Sunday	29
Maundy Thursday	30
Maundy Thursday 2 – We rise	31
Good Friday	32
Holy Saturday	33

Easter
Raised to life	34
Heartlock	35
The Pruning	36
To love	37

Ordinary Time
Daybreak	38
Firstborn	39
From the mouth	39
Enough	40
Moses on Sinai	41
On Pisgah	42
The Prophet I	43
The Prophet II	43
'Til death us do part	44
Amidst the Ruins	44
Scorched lips	45

Offence	46
Wordless	46
The Prophet III	47
And you shall lose your life to find it	47
Blessed are those who mourn	48
Rock to sand	49
The table heaves	50
Who has not suffered an impediment of speech?	51
See these stones	51
Like Bartimeus, I want to see	52
The clutch for meaning	53
The one thing, the better part	53
Bent over	54
Lost and Found	55
Confidence misplaced	55
Outsiders	56
Some yearnings are so deep	57
The grateful eye	57
Am I lost?	58
I stand	58
Word Becomes Flesh	59

Part 2 Gathering Up Grace — 65

The Geography of Grief

The Tom Cycle	66
Organ Failure	73
Things my father gave to me	75
Weather Talk (for my father)	76
The most beautiful thing	77
Last rites	79
Death's undoing	80
Grief's Pool	81
For my mother	82
Stardust	83

On the Road
The Storm	85
Go to your cell	86
The Vow	88
Sea Wind	89
Blood Donation	90
What if?	91
Breathe	91
It slips between my fingers	92
Earthing	93
I am not satisfied	93
On the road	94
Kintsugi (Gathering the Fragments)	95
Beginner's Mind	97
Redemption Road	98
Vocation Prayer	99
Endurance	99
Sunday morning	100
The Sea	101
Grace is Grace. It comes.	102
Walking with Sophia	103
Coming Home	104
Now	105
Meditation on *Tarn Beck Falls in Winter Spate*	106
In wonder	106

New Psalms and Prayers
Psalm for the Newly Born	107
Psalm for the Seed	108
Harvest Psalm	109
Woodland Wedding Psalm	110
Psalm for the Dead	112
Psalm of Praise	113
Psalm of Lament	114
Psalm of Rest	115
Ode to Courage	116

Prayer for Awakening I	117
Prayer for Awakening II	117
Prayer for the start of a new week	118
Prayer of Thanksgiving for Enduring Love	119
Mother's Day Prayer	120
Strong Prayer	121
Divine Sex	121
Song for Petticoe Wick	122

The Way of St Cuthbert – poems and prayers
A prayer for beginning a journey	123
Prayer for a long day	124
Prayer for ascent	124
A prayer to enter the wilderness	125
Prayer among the Cheviots	126
A pilgrim prayer	127
A prayer for journey's end (a new beginning)	129

Scripture Index   130

To the Reader

I write to save my life. The drama of that statement startles me. But there have been times when it has felt literally true. The lectionary poems in Part 1 *Wrestling the Word* and the poems in *On the Road* and *The Geography of Grief* in Part 2 *Gathering Up Grace* are those kinds of poems. They are poems that I started writing as and when my life fell apart. The violent death of my brother, followed by the quick death of my father and the more prolonged of my mother (they said Tom's death would kill them) – all accompanied by an increasingly confusing and assumption-shattering few years in my work – left my brain in pieces. The world as I knew it became threatening and frightening. Nothing measured up. I couldn't do numbers (as I discovered when I later tried to find documents I had filed by date). I couldn't do people, couldn't even look them in the eye. I couldn't continue the work I had always found life-giving even when challenging. So I left ministry and swapped the pulpit for the pew or a Sunday morning walk.

Truth be told, I was tempted to leave the church too. Having lost my compassion and discovered the limitations and shadow side of some Christian traditions, what was left? The first few months after I left ministry, I could scarcely bear to hear of God's love or God's desire that we love. I was too traumatized to receive or to give anything. I did not understand what had happened to me and could neither seek nor find comfort or guidance. A few things were clear: I needed to be in my body – moving, singing, dancing, walking, swimming. I needed to be outdoors, beneath a big sky. And I needed, sometimes, to write.

What the poems reveal is that, although I felt myself to be

leaving a past life, the Holy had no intention of leaving me. Grace kept leaking under the lintel and seeping over the sill of my closed heart-door, presenting itself in all kinds of weird and wonderful ways: an invitation to learn and teach about trauma, the welcome of wild women singers, the hearty company of North Sea swimmers and, as ever, the steadfast love of family and friends.

I am happy to report that my compassion came back as I walked, danced, sang, swam, studied and especially as I cared for my mother as she died. Judy Grosch was a love; just about everyone took to her. I adored her. My natural compassion came from her, and it started to come back to me as I lived in her world for two months to accompany her Home. It took a few more years for a full recovery, years during which I learned to listen in new ways to the Holy and to my bodyself. As with most things, I learn the hard way. I regret that when others are involved.

So *Lifelines* is about the mystery at the heart of Christian faith: that a seed falls into the earth and dies in order for new life to rise up. Summed up in a sentence it appears palatable, almost trite. But the journey can be arduous and take longer than one cycle of seasons.

This book is in two parts. *Wrestling the Word* roots the reality of the journey in the sacred stories that have shaped Christian life for centuries. *Gathering Up Grace* is the worthy effort to name and claim the presence of the ineffable even amid the ruins, ultimately celebrating the triumph of resilient love.

The Parts

Wrestling the Word does what it says on the tin. These poems explore and celebrate the struggling and striving endeavour of reading the Bible in the context of twenty-first-century Britain. In my reading of the text I am always seeking the deeper truths, divine and human, that transcend the cultures in which the Bible came into existence. In the seventeenth century Francis Bacon observed that God revealed Godself in the Word (the Bible) and in the created World. While he warned against mingling these two unwisely, I find that both are essential to make sense of where we find ourselves today and what God – the cohering power that holds the universe together and strives towards the flourishing of all life – may be desiring for us.

The first poem *Genesis* speaks to the origin of my writing, that it is a longing and an offering.

What follows this poem is a collection of poems and prayers that arise from wrangling the Sunday lectionary. When I swapped the pulpit for the pew, I found myself using the sermon time – ear half-cocked to the preacher – to discover where the Word was landing in my life. For decades walking into the church on Sunday morning has been an encounter with who and how I really am. Standing before God strips one of defences; there is nowhere to hide. The witness of these poems is of a soul searching for an earthed faith that makes sense of life.

The lengthy prose poem that ends Part 1 is best performed. Entitled *Word Becomes Flesh*, it is a rendering of the Bible in narrative form that comes to what may be a surprising conclusion for some. The gist of my argument is that the Word creates worlds, God's method being conversation not coercion. It is a plea for the kind of care-filled listening that bridges divides and imagines life-giving possibilities. It dares all of us to love the earth, the Other and ourselves as God does.

Part 2, *Gathering Up Grace*, is a collection of poems and prayers, some charting the difficult journey, some pure celebration. These poems are classed in subsections: *The Geography of Grief*, *On the Road*, *New Psalms and Prayers* and *The Way of St Cuthbert*. *The Geography of Grief* is a charting of the devastation and disorientation that followed the particular deaths of my brother and parents. In the particulars one witnesses the seismic shifts death brings. *On the Road* maps the winding way of losing and finding life and faith in the longer aftermath. *New Psalms* celebrate life moments: the birth of a child, a wedding, harvest, even death. The Psalms in our Bible can be divided into five books, as they are in the Jewish Scriptures *Tanakh*, each one deriving from a different period in Israel's life. Each book reflects a specific time period when they were put together to respond to what was happening. It is a testament to the fulsomeness of the psalms that the Christian community accepted them as is; a broad scope of human life is expressed in the collection. Yet different times and places elicit different songs. *New Psalms* are an offering for our time. Finally, the *Way of St Cuthbert* prayers chart the journey from Melrose through the Borders and into the Cheviots, ending with a barefoot walk to Holy Island, a pilgrimage of body and soul.

I offer these words to you in case they may serve as a lifeline, a revelation, or a sharing in joy or terror, with my prayers.

Carla A. Grosch-Miller
Northumberland, 2019

Genesis

It begins with
   longing.

The heart seeks
words to
hold its desire,
words to
leap the chasm
between I and Thou,
words drawn
from the centre depths,
that become flowers
held
in an open hand,

an offering.

PART 1

Wrestling the Word

Lectionary Poems
Advent
Christmas
Epiphany
Lent
Easter
Ordinary Time

Welcome.
Come well, come ill.
Come sorrowing, come joyful.

Just come.

Come to life that knows of death.
Come to peace that shoulders
 pain.

Just come.

Come hungry, come thirsty.
Come young, come old.

Come.

Advent

The Waiting

Come now the winter,
cold and dark.
Come now the waiting.

Know this:
Salvation is on its way,
to be seen only
glancing backwards.

It will surprise you.

One knows not its form
or its ways:
what must fall
   from one's grasp,
what must break,
what must be endured

so that life,
newborn
and shining,
may come.

The Tender Shoot

What tender shoot
pushes
greenly
through frosty soil?

What song,
buried in earth's womb,
tests its virgin voice
on the wind?

Now is the time
of awakened watching,
of sheltering and sighing,
of cherishing seeds of possibility.

For we know:
every bud does not flower.
Only those nourished by hope
and nurtured with courage
dare to bloom,

their beauty
first imagined
in the heart
of God.

The Call to Repent

Strange comfort this –
a call to repentance.
The requirement of self-examination
before throwing the stone
that breaks an uneasy peace.

(Is every peace uneasy?
A compromise?
A tension held by trembling hands?
Will true peace
forever escape our grasp?)

This waiting season counsels patience
and incites preparation.
Raise the valleys, bring low the mountains:
Level the playing field.
The angels are listening.

Those of high estate face their delusion,
breath evaporating on mirror.
Those of low estate feel the tender
touch that lifts despair.
The labourers give thanks for steady hands.

There is a shining in the grove,
the sound of water splashing.
The way of peace prepared
by humble adoration of a power
well beyond what we can know or claim.

Our skin dripping, we desire
the baptism of Spirit that promises
the end of regret, not knowing
the cost of our freedom
or the necessity of regret.

For we are baptized into love
in this watery death that is a birth.
Love begins in longing and begets loss.
Whoever will love must risk regret
and rise to risk again and again.

Isaiah 40.1–11; Mark 1.1–8; Luke 3.7–18

Leaping

A leap of faith
is called forth.

Into the
   unknown,
abandoning
fear.

My heart
   leaps,
my womb
   sings.

Flying free,
I am.

Luke 1.26–38

The Joseph Cycle

1.

It was the first time I dreamed of –
　　what? God?
The presence was sure but fleeting,
something I glimpsed
as if from the corner of my eye,
　　a glancing backside,
　　a fluttering of angel wings.
I saw it and I knew:
I was to marry her.

I awoke and the image scattered
　　like startled birds,
but the knowing remained.
I was to marry *her*.

I am a simple man.
I work with my hands.
I know wood better than women.
I am sure with the hammer and lathe;
I can measure a beam
　　to a fingerbreadth's accuracy
with only my eye.
I work with the grain, not against it.
The rules that order the world
order my work; it would be foolish
to ignore them.

And yet …
And yet …
I am to marry her.

I turn the words around in my mind;
try to get the weight and measure of them,
test their resilience as I would a beam,
and test my own.

2.

I am to marry her.
I didn't see that coming.

But I find,
    as I sit with that sentence,
the words take on
a life of their own. I see us

years down the road,
this little one learning to hold
the reed and work the lathe;
Mary, whilst cradling another bairn,
sighing over the first crude
creation from his hands
as if it were heaven born.

I see the warmth of our hearth
and feel the comfort of her arms.
I swell with pride to see the lad grow.

Who knows what life
will hold for him?
Who knows what my choice
to be his father will give to him
or to me?
Who knows?

3.

I heard, too,
be not afraid.
As Mary heard.

As if we could lay fear
down; as if
we should.
If this is God's plan,

if God has a hand
on our shoulders,
we should be afraid.

The Holy comes with
no guarantee of ease,
no promise of safety.
The streets of Jerusalem are littered
with silent memorials to prophets
stoned; the words of their
mouths hanging in the air long past
their utterance,
    like the Roman crosses lining
    the road to the city,
a reminder of the cost of
doing business with God.

Is this to be my boy's fate?

Why then do I feel peace
as I let the words
marry her weave
an indissoluble bond
between
she and I,
him and me?

Matthew 1.18–25

Meditation on Rembrandt's
The Holy Family by Night
(a scene in the family workshop/home)

Not always delicate, this craft.
But even seemingly clumsy choices
create beauty.

It is the effort that is essential.
The attendance to detail,
to what is necessary.

A risk-taking,
breath-holding
endeavour.

Matthew 1.18–25

Expectant

A thirsty land
    implores heaven.
A child leaps
in utero.

Expectant,
we await
good news.

Luke 1.39–45

Christmas

Christmas Eve

This Christmas
I ache for your birth
as never before.

My heart has been cracked
open, its pain laid bare.

Even the earth is flayed and bleeding;
the hot throb of human desire
melts icecaps.

Only the babe's cry will
dispel the fear and despair
that have clung so closely,
clogged our hearts,
blinkered our vision.

Come, little one.

I would stand
on the hillside
scanning the skies
every night given me
to catch a glimpse,
 the blur of an angel wing,
the shimmering song
of heaven echoing
my deepest longing.

And I would cradle that song.
I would let it fill my throat and my heart
the rest of my days.

Christmas Morn

A burst of joy,
a bundle of love,
a heart overflowing.
Thanks be to God.

You deign to make your home
among us, we complicated dust,
we frail, fallible fools,
we self-obsessed buffoons.

What wonder is this?
What incomprehensible joy?

The Slaughter of Innocence

When was your innocence slaughtered?
And have you picked up the gossamer pieces
    and made something beautiful and strong and
yours with them?

They say 'time heals all wounds'.
My mother would say 'time wounds all heels'.
But the truth lies elsewhere.

No alchemy this, but
we become strong and wise
in the broken places.

The shimmering veil
ripped to shreds
makes silk threads to
weave a shroud,
a shawl,
a shelter,
a song.

Matthew 2.13–18

Song of a Mother

I asked,
I received,
I gave.

By a miracle my womb opened,
and life emerged, fresh as dew,
bloodstained and downy.

The time now is marked not by longing,
but by the daily tasks of tending to life:
holding,
feeding,
watching.

From before conception,
love has laboured to make this life possible.
Now I bend my back to the tasks –
absorbed in the moment
with willing hands and open heart,
alive to the time when this life
will stand in the Presence,
utter his longing
and offer his life.

So the dance of life goes on:
longing and offering
the rhythm, graced steps
the warp and weft of love

woven by many hands
and one Heart.

1 Samuel 1.20–28; Luke 2.33–35

Epiphany

Star of Wisdom

The guiding star
   a corresponding wonder,
   a resonance,
   a knowing.

An assurance
   and a joy.

No truer compass,
No more trustworthy a map.

Let wonder lead …

Matthew 2.1–12

Baptism of Jesus

It was a baptism of
   fire and of ice,
   of power and of passion
melding heaven and earth,
forging strength, summoning
untold possibilities.

An awakening
   opening eyes
that would no longer
   be able to unsee.

A choice, a *Yes*
unleashing challenge and grace
in equal measure.

Matthew 3.13–17; Mark 1.4–11; Luke 3.15–17, 21–22

The Tree

Rooted in earth,
nourished and held fast,
I stretch my branches to the sky.

Come summer, I fruit.
Come winter, I rest.

When the wind rises,
I dance and sway.
When the rain ceases,
I send tendrils deep.
When storms rage,
I grip earth harder.

I bear the snap of dead wood.
I tingle to bud and glory to flower.

When it is my time,
I will return to earth
to feed and strengthen others.

So I live,
   and die to live again.

Psalm 1; Jeremiah 17.5–10

The Call

It was an ordinary day.
Unremarkable skies,
gull squawk and squabble filling the air,
sun squinting off gentle waves.
My hands busy with the nets,
    mending, testing, coiling.

Nothing suggested a day
unlike any other.

Consumed in my tasks,
    making ready,
I thoughtlessly glanced up.

There he stood.

It was not this or that.
I cannot put my finger on it.
But somehow, in that glance,
everything changed for me.

Some longing was touched,
    some deep knowing,
and I could not rest

until I turned my hand
from mending nets
to mending the world.

Matthew 4.12–25

Make Peace

Give with a peaceful heart,
   a reconciled heart,
  a heart that knows its worth,
     that gives freely without expectation
     or regard for how the gift will be
received.

Give with a peaceful heart,
   a simple heart,
  a humble heart
     one desirous and able to
     listen, a heart open to other
hearts.

Give with a peaceful heart,
   a wise heart,
  a care-full heart,
     a heart broken and healed
     and aware that it will break
again.

Matthew 5.21–37

Becoming

We grow into who
we are to become.

A seed is sown;
the days unfold.

In the seed,
there is a song ...
a faint pulse
growing stronger.

Warmth of sun,
freshness of rain,
moonlight and starlight,
the green of grass and trees,
the flight of birds

teach notes
and invite
an open throat

to sing life
into being.

Jeremiah 1.4–10

In the Footsteps of Elijah

The whirlwind looms;
a tornado has been sighted.
All is at risk.

I walk towards it,
my blood turning to ice.

The wind whistles;
I strain to hear
'I will not leave you.'

Silence engulfs me,
its walls made of cloud.
I see no farther
than my hand
pressed up against
the soundless fog.

My breath deepens.
My pulse accelerates,
then slows.
I note tightness
in my chest.

I take a step,
my hand on my robe,
ready to rend it
and stand naked
before The Storm.

1 Kings 19

Holy

Holy are you, O God,
and holy is your name.

My tongue falls mute.

I am a seashell tossed on the beach,
open to wind and wave,
an infinitesimally small part
of a vast and wondrous universe.

In my smallness,
I am surrounded
by your immensity.

In my stillness,
I am enfolded
in your silence.

In my emptiness,
I am filled
with your grace.

Holy are you, O God,
and holy is your name.

Leviticus 19.1–2

The Radiance!

The radiance! The radiance!
No mere spark
but the fullness of light.

My vision will never be the same.

Retinas forever scarred,
the memory of light
will haunt me
until the end
of my days.

It will tempt me to risk,
to climb again, daring high footfall,
to see – if only in my mind's eye –
The glory! The glory!
and to let it fill the whole of me.

Mark 9.2–9

Lent

Wild Beasts

Some wilderness, this.

A warm home.
Time away from
the pressing of crowds.
Clearing the space
to listen to my life.

Wild beasts, there are.
The primordial urge to make my mark.
Fear of a future unknown.
The freedom and burden of choice.
The wound of death.

The wound of death,
the slash of a wild beast.
The wound of death,
ripping the veil from my eyes.
The wound of death,
calling me to the joy
and terror that is life.

Thanks be to God for the wild beasts,
as much as for the ministrations of angels.
Indeed, cursed be those ministrations
that prematurely bandage
the revealing of
the wound of death.

Banish the angels, then,
who come of their own need.

Send me only the Silence
that reveals the wound
in all its glory.

Mark 1.12–13

For the Leader *(Nicodemus)*

To lead is
to listen,
to watch and
to wonder.

To lead is
to question,
to probe and
to ponder.

To lead is
to humble
self over
and over.

To lead is
to let the
Wind gather
and scatter.

To lead is
to know of
the things that
most matter.

John 3.1–17

Sarah Speaks

Old as dirt, I was,
when the Fire asked
me to come near.

Weary as dust, I was,
when the Possible whispered
an impossible promise
in my ear.

An old woman's dreams,
what can they matter
to the Breath
at the Heart
of the All?

I have heard other whispers,
believed six impossible things
before breakfast,
trusted my own wits and will,
and bear the scars
to prove it.

Why listen to this one?

I have risked life and limb,
learned too many things
the hard way,
wrestled the Real
and come away limping
but blessed.

Why risk now?
Why not?

I scan the words,
looking for the devil's mark:

the appeal to vainglory,
to power, to position.
And I find it.
There amongst the longing
for a lasting home
and the desire to hold
the fruit of one's womb
in one's arms.

The Holy and the Unholy
are as interwoven
as wheat and tares.

As it was in the beginning,
is now and ever shall be.

Genesis 17.1–16

Temptation

Driven to the desert
   windswept
   heartweary

The hidden exposed
   uncouth desires
   base drives

Old Eve

Mark 1.9–15

Ode to Moses' Mum

Years of making baskets stood her in good stead.
Hands firm, she wove the strands of sedge tightly,
every pull a prayer.
Tree sap and bitumen to strengthen the seal
her Amen.

She thought her heart would break
as she laid the wee bairn in it.
His belly full, his bow lips pursed,
dark lashes resting on soft cheeks.
He knew nothing of the dangers ahead.
Final kiss on his brow, she gave the basket
to his strong, brave sister.

Then the long wait. Every breath a prayer.
Minutes stretching to hours.
Until
joy erupted, filling every longing emptiness,
with the sound of his hungry cry
and the sight of Miriam's triumphant face.

Her swollen breasts leaking, the bairn
latched and rooted and suckled
and she was filled.

In the weeks, months and years that followed,
whenever he was in her arms
she whispered *I am*
in his ears, filling his small head
with the stories of his people,

stories that became a woven basket
for his and the people's hopes and dreams,
every pull a prayer.
Cuddles and kisses to strengthen the seal
her Amen.

Exodus 2.1–10

There is a time

There is a time for rules,
wisdom writ in plain language
that memory might be preserved.

And there is a time for mercy,
the gentle bending of law
at wisdom's request.

There is a time for rage,
violation's marker
speaking up for pain.

And there is a time for reflection,
the tender holding of hurt
for lessons learned.

There is a time for certainty,
clear focus driving
resolute action.

And there is a time for unknowing,
soft protection for seeds
unready to face full sun.

Exodus 20.1–17; John 2.13–22

Hidden Depths

Deep truths
pulse and flow
beneath the surface
of daily life.

Any small crack allows
them to break into view,
to startle
and resonate.

They are cloaked in mystery;
we stare and stammer,
unable to wrap words
around the reality revealed.

We close our eyes to rest;
the brilliance does not abate.
We are never more alive
than in this moment.

Songs and symbols,
prayer and praise
seek to focus our gaze,
sharpen our sight.

In time we come to know:
grasping and clinging
pervert truth.

We must let go
and open ourselves
to the great ebb and flow,
the glimmer

and the startling resonance
that are our salvation.

1 Corinthians 1.18–31

Dying to life

Perhaps the old form of faith
must die, fall into the dust
and return to its beginning
that new life, freed and unfettered,
may rise.

Perhaps the tomb is naught to fear,
the darkness an unravelling,
a comfort and a rest.

Perhaps light comes stealthily,
and garments become threadbare,
and radiance grows from within.

Perhaps the great letting go is a letting be,
an acceptance and a grace,
that life may spring up,
radiance meeting radiance,
wonder comprehending wonder.

John 11.1–45

Also printed in Ruth Burgess, *Spring* (Glasgow: Wild Goose Publications, 2019), pp. 282–3. Original copyright retained by Carla A. Grosch-Miller.

Passion Sunday

A palm parade snakes
through white slab graves
on the Mount of Olives,
glancing the garden
that will soon hear
anguished prayer.

So begins the holy week
where humanity's heart is exposed
in tenderness of touch and scheming,
patient witness and betrayal,
courage and desertion,
sight and blindness.

The line between love and hatred
so fine, so easily crossed.

Maundy Thursday

What love is this?
That stoops and serves
That greets betrayal
That fears no evil.

See the hands, calloused and tender,
take each foot, wash it gently.
Embarrassed eyes look away
but still receive the touch.

Each one hungry for love
one way or another.
Each one's longing revealed
in a dusty foot.

What is stronger:
tender touch
or spoken word?
What will linger
in the memory,
in the body's cells?
What moulds the will
and sparks the act?

Cry glory!
Glory for the one
who kneels
before he stands.
Glory for the one
whose hands caress
the unlovely.
Glory for the one
who would rather die
than leave us
untouched,
unmoved.

John 13.1–17, 31b–35

Maundy Thursday 2 – We rise

Unleavened bread
made in a hurry –
no time to rise.

The memory of bread on our lips,
laden with grief and fear,
spurred on by hunger for freedom,
   we rise.

Our eyes fixed on the horizon,
not knowing what lies ahead;
small comforts left behind,
   we rise.

Matthew 26.17–20, 26–30

Good Friday

The chattering birds
   feed on electric tension,
   prepare to settle
   for the worst of it,
come to stillness.

We can scarce take it in,
   neuter searing words
   with singsong delivery,
   attempt explanation,
   leap to the coming triumph,
don't want to stay
in the difficult place.

All we are asked,
   all that is needful,
is to dwell in silence
before the unfolding horror,
the death of meaning,
the end of hope.

Stay here.
Face the widening abyss.
Feel the contours of
   the spreading darkness.

Holy Saturday

I stand at the garden tomb,
its silence complete
but for the song of the nightingale.

If heaven's gate is opened,
the wound of death still stings.
No balm in stone;
the desertion of friends
almost a comfort.

Time and space
suspend.
The unthinkable
is.

I am hollow
yet
more alive
than ever
I was
on the road.

Easter

Raised to life

earthquake cracked
stones catch tears
of sorrow and joy

what has died
shall never be
forgotten,
and through the cracks,

first the leaf
and then the lily
shall appear.

Heartlock

My heart locked,
You found ways in.

You leaked human kindness under the lintel,
dripped hope through the keyhole,
poured possibility over the threshold.

You shoved love letters
through the mail box.

Slowly,
I remembered.

I remembered who I am
in the depth of my being.

I heard again,
in the speaking of my name,
a call to life.

My heart, warmed,
opened like a spring bud.

Luke 24.36–48

The Pruning

Dead wood, this,
this naivety, this sureness, this futile fantasy.
Cut it off.

And this,
this arrogance, this thoughtless carelessness.
Snap it.

Not all is lost,
not all is dead.

The green will come,
a brave leaf unfurl,
   rising and ready
    for the summer dance.

Then, at the right time,
golden at dusk,
it will surrender itself to soil,

death a nourishment
for life to come.

John 15.1–18

To love

To love is to dwell
to attend, to be fully present
to open one's heart
    to who and what is.

To love is to risk
to enter the reality of pain, even death
to stand or sit, breathless, a witness
    to weep.

To love is to soar
to chance upon the pearl
to wonder at the blaze of sunset
    to live.

To love is to release
to glimpse the veil rent
to receive the gift of here, now
    to be.

John 14.23–29

Ordinary Time

Daybreak

Day begins to break
   the orange glow on the horizon
   hopeful, a creeping warmth.

Blood surges into muscles,
   insistent, willing a final push
   to prevail.

I will wrest a blessing
from this long struggle.

And though the memory and the wound
will endure and shape my walk
for the rest of my days,

in the facing up and the leaning in,
in the wrestling and the letting go,

I will be blessed.

I will own my name.

Genesis 32.22–32

'Daybreak' was first published in *Practical Theology* vol. 10, no.1, p. 47 (March 2017). It is reprinted by kind permission of Taylor & Francis Ltd.

Firstborn

Firstborn	fastborn	itchy feet	born to leave
fast	impatient	wandering star	to love
faster	fingers thrum wood	pushing boundaries	and to leave
born to run	legs swing	escape	freeborn

Genesis 21.1–21

From the mouth

What comes out of the mouth
comes from the heart.

A plea for help,
   desperate cry,
is an act of faith.

A cry to crack the heart open.

Our common humanity
the conduit of grace.

Matthew 15.10–28

Enough

When I wanted to lie down
on the graves of my parents,
next to my brother

When I held my head in my hands,
despairing and hurting,
unable to heal myself

When I opened my hands and let go
of almost all I held dear,
releasing it, stepping away

You kneaded the bread,
fired the oven
and marshalled the angels
to prepare to drop manna
just when and where I needed it.

Just enough,
each day,
just enough.

Which was the only way
I could accept it.

Enough to honour
my freedom.
Enough to feed me
and lead me home.

Exodus 16.2–15

Moses on Sinai

I've been here before
Here – where you first caught my attention.

The memory of fire has never left me,
nor the feel of stone on bare feet,
the shock of recognition
at the sound of my own name,
the dawning realization
that my lonely, sheep-filled days were numbered.
You, I AM, were calling me to a different way of life.

Here I am, now,
not quite wizened by the years gone by.
Winded by the long climb, moved again
by the sight of mountains upon mountains
stretching to the horizon,
I remove my sandals once more,
that I may feel your power come up from the earth.

The air is clear here.
I breathe deeply, lift my head
and catch your sweet and chastening song.

We are given all we need.

What we do with it
is up to us.

Exodus 19; 20

On Pisgah

A lifetime of scrambling towards holiness was to end here,
amidst a crowd of clouds and the perfect patience
of mountains carved by unseen hands,
a blaze of light breaking through slate grey skies,
mist rising from green sloped rock.

The dream of the promised land burned
onto the back of his eyelids,
he will die in hope.
While we,
scorched by holy fire,
resume the scramble,
lose our footing,
stop to catch our breath,
bruise our shins,
and toss restlessly in our beds,
hoping and praying
for the assurance
of things unseen.

I too would stand at Pisgah,
let hope sear my heart
and a vision of glory
burn the inside of my eyelids.
I too would gladly spend my days
trudging, slipping, sliding, scaling,
scrape my knees,
offer my hands to rock to tear,
let beauty break and bind my heart
that I might glimpse true holiness.

Let the Adversary depart from these heights,
its promises splintering on eternal peaks,
and let the angels come to minister in kindness.

For in the end there is only kindness
that hearkens to the kingdom of heaven.

Deuteronomy 34; Matthew 4
Published in *Reform* (the magazine of the United Reformed Church)
in 2015; reprinted with kind permission.

The Prophet I

Go out,
stand on the mountain.
Let wind batter you.
Witness a roil of clouds.
Drink in beauty
and terror.
Glimpse eternity.

Know.

1 Kings 19.8–13a

The Prophet II

The storm rages within and outwith.
   Surroundsound strikes terror,
   pyrotechnics paralyse.
The earth shudders.

Then – a breath.
Silence that enters the bones,
strengthens sinews,
knits together brokenness
   in deep places,
renews heart.

I arise,
ready.

1 Kings 19.8–13a

'Til death us do part

My hand, still warm, will clutch yours as yours grows cold.
My love, a bridge, will carry you as you cross the waters.
My breath, a prayer, will sing you all the way Home.

2 Kings 2.1–12

Amidst the Ruins

We search for your purpose
in the ruins around us.

We strain to see you
through eyes clouded by tears.

We struggle to hear you
amidst the clamouring
of the dispossessed.

God,
persistent as the winter wind,
enduring as the summer sun,
melt our assumptions with your mercy.
Stretch our minds towards your horizons.
And enable us to live these difficult days,
believing seeds wait for the right time
to spring to life.

Isaiah 45.1–7

Scorched lips

My lips burn.
The searing heat of words
   spoken in fear
scorched the earth
and set my lips on fire.

There is no flame
that does not burn
innocent and guilty
alike.

A horrified apology
stutters through blisters.
It hangs in the air
and is batted away
by clenched fists.

My throat chokes on the ashes.
I am thrust down to the ground
to eat the dirt of humility.

And, not for the last time,
   dust and ashes
   clinging to my tongue,
I taste the power of fear
to hurt, pervert and maim,
to burn and burn
and burn
again.

At ground level,
I breathe the humus of being
and offer my broken
fearful heart
to the scarred hands
of Love
that will not let me go.

Isaiah 6.1–8

Offence

It is easy to dismiss
   the wounds of others,
to close our eyes
   to the hollow hunger
   of the hopeless,
to turn our heads
   and turn off our tellies

avoiding the offence of floating bodies,
desperate or dead.

Jeremiah 8.4–9.1

Wordless

A famine of the Word.
No greater desolation.
Eyes blind to beauty.
Ears deaf to birdsong.
Heart dead to wonder.

For what is the Word
but a signpost to the Presence
that lights day and night,
coaxes life from seed and autumn to loam,
that breathes in you and me

and leads us into love.

Amos 8

The Prophet III

Write the vision
Make it plain
That she may run who reads it

Paint the picture
Make it shine
That he may dance who glimpses it

Sing the song
Make it loud
That they may shout who hear it

Habakkuk 2

And you shall lose your life to find it;
   hours you shall lose, days, even years.
Though lost to you, these stricken times
   are not lost.
Deep within, unspoken forces are at work,
   creating
   not order
   but beauty.

Only the lost know what it is to be found.
Only those who have lost,
   who have peered into the abyss, raised a fist to the sky
   and stuck out a limb to be pruned,
   whose hand has become practised at letting go ...
those are able to sway and bend,
   leafing in spring,
   fearless in winter.

Matthew 16.21–28

Blessed are those who mourn

Blessed are those who mourn,
   who have loved at depth
   who feel the pain of loss
     as an arrow piercing the heart
   who do not know how
they will rise to a new day.

Blessed are those who mourn,
   who wail and rend their clothes
   who sit in the dust and weep
     as a flood ravages a ravine
   who say the unsayable and
who will rise to a new day.

Blessed are the raw cries of the wounded,
   the tears of the forlorn,
   the hollowing, hallowing sound
     of the silence which begins
   the long night before
the rising of a new day.

Blessed are the living and blessed are the dead.
Those who mourn know the power of love
in life gone before and life rising to a new day.

Matthew 5.1–12

Rock to sand

We forget –
   in time
   all rock
   becomes
sand.

Flood and fire,
wind and rain
are not enemies
but agents
of the Real:
   revealing,
   refining,
   remaking.

Open my heart
to the great and subtle
flow of water and wind
that will
   reveal,
   refine
   and
   remake
me.

Matthew 7.24–27

The table heaves
with the bounty of the earth.
The invitation is to all.

But there is a cost.

The guests must ensure
that those less able
will be able
to belly up to the bounty.

Yes to God is
Yes to enough for all.

Yes to God is
Yes to the earth.

Yes to God is
Yes to life.

Matthew 22.1–14

Who has not suffered an impediment of speech?
Who has not said that which cannot be unspoken,
   that which benefits no one and nothing,
     which hurts and harms, decimates and devastates?

Who has not suffered hardness of hearing?
Who has not turned away from words that must be spoken,
   words carrying the breath of life, the song of the soul,
     the seeds of a new day?

Swollen of tongue, rigid of ear,
what healing touch will restore us?

Mark 7.31–37

See these stones

The mortar is crumbling already,
grit crunches beneath the feet.
This wall will fall.
In time they all do.
The earth takes back her own.
It is all hers.

Small holes in the wall,
   like hotel room spyholes,
offer insufficient purchase
to what's on the other side.
Tomorrow is not within our grasp,
   certainly not in our control.
Though surely our actions and failures bring it on.

Standing in the ruins,
our vision momentarily sharp,
we wonder.

Mark 13.1–8

Like Bartimeus, I want to see.

I want to see,
to stand with my mouth agape
   on the mountain top and in the valley,
   in field and forest,
   seaside and streamside,
astounded at the wonder of creation.

I want the veil to drop.

I want to open the fridge,
see the plastic yogurt pots
and know their destiny –
   a landfill,
   a belching incinerator,
   a river,
   an island of plastic floating in the ocean.

I want to see into the hearts of others
and to know the impact of
   my gaze,
   my words,
   my actions,
   my omissions.

I want to use my car, my ipad, my television
and to know the impact on
   the environment,
   workers around the world,
   my own mind and character.

I want to see,

   and to have
   the courage,
   the wisdom
   and the patience
to bear what I see.

Mark 10.46–52

The clutch for meaning
The grasp for a firm handrail,
   a strong foothold.

But truth, like water,
   like air,
flows through our fingers.

Luke 8.9–10; Mark 4.10–12

The one thing, the better part,
is never taken away.
It is the pearl of great price,
the treasure that moth and rust
do not consume.

Call it a sense of belonging to the cosmos,
the grateful acceptance of being
and being at home
   in one's skin
   on this earth
   with these people.

Call it humility.
Call it wonder.
Call it love.

Luke 10.38–42

Bent over

Still I come,
carrying the hurts and confusions,
fear and anger,
the weight of which bend me over,
make it hard for me to meet
the eye of a stranger.
The friendliest face hides enmity
that reveals itself over time.

Still I come
to this holy place,
perhaps to be reminded
that there is the potential
and the power
for me to one day
stand to praise.

So I come,
as do others,
in fear and in hope,
to taste freedom's sweetness
and let it linger on the tongue,
looking to the time
when I shall be
emptied of all but love.

Luke 13.10–17

Lost and Found

This loss confounds me.

I'm not even sure what's gone
but all the bits it held together
have scattered on the floor,
rolled under the stove
and dived into the cracks
between the boards.

I'm minded to let them lie
so long as they don't trip me up
– which they might.
And they should.

How else will I come to know
what's been lost
and what can be found.

Luke 15.1–10

Confidence misplaced,
Queen of all I survey.

But the unseen,
   the unknown,
is greater.

How quickly we fall.

Luke 18.9–14

Outsiders

Those who stand on the outside,
who did not grow up
breathing the air of this place,
see more.

Bereft of fellows,
but not of fellow feeling,
they catch the kind and the cruel
and are moved by both.

What is faith but to notice,
to intercede, to give thanks?

Our full humanity is called forth
by the face of the other.

Luke 17.11–19

Some yearnings are so deep –
>   the skin's hunger for touch
>   the self's desire to love and be loved
>   the soul's longing to sing her own song
>   the thirst for justice
>   born of the heart's tenderness
>   the eyes' recognition of another
>   the hope of reconciliation
>   the ache for healing.

Some yearnings are so deep
that they will
>   break through the wrecked rubble
>   of destroyed buildings
>   burst out of cracks in concrete
>   tear the veil of fear and worry
to seek and to find
what is necessary for life.

Luke 18.1–18

The grateful eye sees beauty.
The grateful heart beholds goodness.
The grateful mind contemplates in awe.
The grateful hand shares.
The grateful life bears fruit.

Philippians 4.4–9

Am I lost?
Has your good purpose
been fulfilled
in my life?

Like Zacchaeus,
I long to meet you
and in the encounter
see myself
as I really am.

Heal me of my greed
and take my fear away.

Loose my grip
on all I have

that I may open my hands
to receive the life
you have for me.

Luke 19.1–11; 2 Thessalonians 1.11–2.2

I stand,
   tilt my head back,
   open my throat
and breathe.

Welcome, Holy Spirit,
massage my heart,
warm my blood,
oxygenate my brain.

Shape me for
Your living.

Romans 12.1–9

Word Becomes Flesh
(to be performed with passion)

In the beginning
When the earth was vast and void
Hovering between *is* and *not yet*
The Spirit brooded over the face of the deep
Pregnant with potential
God spoke ...
>   *Let there be light*
And there was light.

From the first phrase, a flood of words followed.
In response: horizons spread,
mountains reached for the sky,
deserts danced to the sea,
sun, moon and stars circled and bowed.
Life erupted in glorious colour and stark contrast, scents
aromatic and repugnant, textures silky and spiky, sounds
melodious and cacophonous, tastes enticing and acrid.
Life, verdant and voluptuous, fecund and fertile,
each thing holding the seed of a future,
is sheltering *not yet*,
the Spirit brooding and birthing at once.

The conversation had begun ...
Each word a partner
Each syllable sharing meaning
Each vowel and consonant shaping reality.

In the torrent of words was one, *ha'adam*,
    earthling, human,
Crafted with love and longing, made in the image of God
    (so we believe, so we aspire).
Ha'adam from *adamah* (earth).
Feet on the earth, thoughts soaring to the sky,
With the power to name and to know,
To choose and to create,
A conversation partner God hoped would be worthy
of the name.

Crafted with love and longing: the sweat of God's brow
mingled with the blood of the human, so that she and he
would always know the salty taste of home,
and they would long for it.
Long for the true and firm hands,
for the sure place of affection
where they could rest and know peace.

Nudging *is* toward *not yet*,
God spoke the words the human needed to hear.

Words of covenant and call:
I will be your God and you will be my people.
Words of blessing and belonging:
*You will be blessed, and in you
all the families of the earth will be blessed.*
Words poised between heaven and earth:
*Your name is Israel, for you have striven
with God and with humans.*
Words that led from slavery to freedom:
*Hear oh Israel, the Lord is your God, the Lord alone.
You shall love the Lord your God with all your heart, and
with all your soul, and with all your might. Keep these words
that I am commanding you in your heart. Recite them to
your children and talk about them when you are at home and
when you are away, when you lie down and when you rise.
Bind them as a sign on your hand, fix them as an emblem
on your forehead, and write them on the doorposts of your
house and on your gates.*

There were more words.
Words of law:
Thou shalt not and *Keep the Sabbath* and
Honour your father and mother.
Words of grace:
*Do not fear, for I have redeemed you;
I have called you by name, you are mine.*

And, always, *remember, remember, remember.*

So the human wrote the words down,
recited them to his children, bound them on her hand.

God continued to speak.

Judges and prophets caught the words on the wind and
shouted them in the streets:
*Share your bread with the hungry, let the oppressed go free,
bring the homeless poor into your house, loose the bonds of
injustice, care for widows and orphans.
Ho, everyone who thirsts, come to the waters; you who have
no money, come, buy and eat.
Listen carefully to me, and eat what is good. Listen, so that
you may live.*

Poets and priests, ears tuned to the silence between the
words, eyes peering into the place where *is* tangos with *not
yet*, wrote songs to lodge in the human heart:
*This is the day that the Lord has made;
let us rejoice and be glad in it.
The Lord is my shepherd, I shall not want.
As a deer pants for flowing streams,
so my soul longs for you, O God.
I lift my eyes to the hills – from where will my help come?
My help comes from the Lord,
who made heaven and earth.*

The supply of words was inexhaustible.
*Day to day pours forth speech, and
night to night declares knowledge.*
The Spirit continued to brood and to birth.

God's desire that the family of *ha'adam* would flourish
conceived another way –
Word made flesh, incarnation, Godself poured into human
flesh that the unseen might be seen, that the ignored might
be compelling, that the vulnerability and strength of love
and life might move hearts and minds, that the conversation
might turn and turn and turn until the family of *ha'adam*
was converted to the power of love through and through.

God had a mission; God's method was conversation:
Word made flesh.

And so the angel visited a young woman, in a small and inconsequential village, and on her
Yes
(God never forces *ha'adam*; God's method is conversation), the Spirit entered her.

And the child Jesus was born in mean estate, homeless and heralded by heavenly host, celebrated by shepherds and stargazers. He dodged the king's rage, fled to Egypt and in due time came home. There he grew from boy to man, felt the heat of the day, roughened his hands in toil, hung on every word that came from the mouth of his Papa, and *became* a clear word, spoken and lived. He lingered in the liminal space between *is* and *not yet*, his heart beating with the knowledge that the reign of God was at hand, within reach. He gathered a motley crew to help him in the tasks at hand, travelled and preached, taught and healed and provoked ... until the time came that the world could not bear his light any more and a fear-filled evil rose up from the bowels of ordinary men and women and killed him.

But that was not the last word.
You can't kill love, the empty tomb whispered.
And the motley crew recognized his scarred hands and feet, and fed him fish and shared his bread, until he ascended with the promise of the Spirit.

Which came like a tornado, raining fire and power. She outdid herself ... unloosed tongues and minds, a clamouring cacophony became a paean of praise to the living God revealed in the Word made flesh. The motley crew appeared drunk with joy, and like some drunks, had a clarity of insight unparalleled before. The crowd was transfixed, perplexed, amazed ... on the power of enfleshed and Spirit-filled words, many put themselves in the flow of that power that very day, as water was poured and *Amen, Alleluia* was shouted on street corners and at riversides.

In heaven there was dancing and celebration. God would pour God's immense love into the frail vessel born that day, as much as its *Yes* would allow, sending it forth to proclaim the good news. God who so loves the world does not, will not, cannot give up on the family of *ha'adam*.
Can a woman forget her nursing child, or show no compassion for the child of her womb? ... See I have inscribed you on the palms of my hands; your walls are continually before me.

God had given the family of *ha'adam* a vision, a picture of a time when lion would lie down with lamb, infants play over the poisonous snake's nest, when *they will not hurt or destroy on all my holy mountain, for the earth will be full of the knowledge of the Lord*; a time of a new heaven and a new earth, when every tear shall be wiped away, and death shall be no more.

The children of *ha'adam* wrote down the words, recited them to their children, bound them in a Book ... living words dancing on the page, bringing life and hope as clear, cool water does in a barren land. Grasped by a new reality, the church gathered around the Book and the table of the Word made flesh, drenched itself in the water and wind of the Spirit, and set about manifesting God's love for the world in the flesh and blood, bricks and mortar of their communities.

Fast forward through the centuries' earnest endeavour, stunning success scarred by pride of power, turbulence of war and gall of dispute, past the power of words to harm and hurt. The time has come for the Word to heal ...

All around the world, bands of faithful contemplate a changing landscape. Above the din of commercial clatter and cynical conversation, amidst competing claims of divine imperative, the call to remember is heard. Small groups gather to hear again the Word, to ingest its immensity, to feast on its fire. Fed with the bread of life, bound together by the Way, swept up into the Spirit, they *dare to love* as

God does – self-giving, unconditionally – across the false boundaries of ethnicity and class and gender and sexual orientation and even theological interpretation. Fearful polarization melts into lively discussion and debate. God has a mission; God's method is conversation! No question is stupid, no discussion off limits. Hospitality is the rule of the day – and there is room for all! Conservative evangelicals dine with gay progressives, each speaking honestly, from the heart, of faith and the struggle to be faithful. Black and white Christians call each other sister and brother, share their joys and their sorrows, own their common humanity. Young and old swap jokes and music, learn each other's dance steps. Spirited worship, reflecting diverse theological perspectives and cultural practices, carries the people into the presence of God and sends them back out again to share the good news.

The people become clear words, spoken and lived, of the power of the living God and the possibility of a reconciled human family. They have learned to live with difference, to honour and respect one another, and carry their ministry of reconciliation into a world that is dying to learn. Leaven enlivening the loaf, goodness spreads throughout the land. The hungry are fed; the poor provided with the means to live. Men and women, and children too, lay down arms and take up listening and learning. Communities scheme the fair sharing of the earth's resources and the protection of the planet. People of all faiths and no faith know they belong to one another and to the earth. Truly, *they shall not hurt or destroy on all my holy mountain.* Prayer and praxis, silence and song, lead the nations to dance to the universal hymn of praise ... and God smiles.

God speaks,
Word becomes flesh,
worlds come into being.

PART 2

Gathering Up Grace

The Geography of Grief
On the Road
New Psalms and Prayers
The Way of St Cuthbert

The Geography of Grief

The Tom Cycle

The day my brother died

The day my brother died
   the phone rang at 3am.
I didn't realize it was the phone –
   these digital-age ringers
   lack intelligibility to sleep-shorn
   ears born in the 1950s –
until I picked it up
and heard my daughter's voice.

The day my brother died
'Uncle Tom's dead' tried to penetrate
the fog that surrounded my brain.
She screamed it three times.
Oh no, I shouted, *no, no.*

The day my brother died
the rain resumed.
Short cloud bursts, longer drizzles
and early morning grey.

The day my brother died
I called my mother.
Her low moan, starting where her womb
used to be, touched the place in me
that fears the worst.
Her gasps and cries sliced through me;
   I knew them.
I have made them myself.
If I live long enough,
I will make them again.

The day my brother died
I called my sister and my sister-in-law.
I called my daughter and my mother again.
(My best friend called me at 7.12am,
   the minute she got my email.)
I tried to believe and not to believe it at the same time.
I tried to do the right thing,
cleared my diary, arranged substitutions.

The day my brother died
it was unreal to me.
As unreal as God.
As unreal as electricity and the internet.
Something in me was cushioning the fall.

The day my brother died
I foreswore my motorcycle.
(He was killed on his.)
I swore I'd never slag anyone off again.
(I'd casually slagged him off to a stranger over the weekend.
Why?)

The day my brother died
as I boarded the bus to work
I almost forgot my socks and my hat.
I did forget: my phone charger, my eye mask, two books.
I also forgot my sense of humour, and my joy.
When the sky turned blue,
I was offended.

The day my brother died
has just begun,
and I sense it will never, ever end.

The day after my brother was cremated

The day after my brother was cremated
I saw a sundog.

The burning happened without us,
    at a big impersonal Los Angeles mausoleum.
No one knew the time, only the date.
They told my sister-in-law 'At the end of the day,
come get the cremains; bring a photo ID.'

The day after my brother was cremated
I swam laps in the pint-sized pool
between the twin towers of a Burbank Holiday Inn.
I had finished 25 laps of breast stroke and turned onto
my back,
my body searching for a sustaining rhythm
and the correct number of strokes to prevent concussion at
pool's end.
I stroked on ... 1, 2, 3, 4 ... watching the blue sky strung
with cirrus wisps
when suddenly I noticed a tricolour refraction through a
bunch of white:
too short for a rainbow, wrong position.
Above the bow a large pine poking through the urban
landscape pierced the sun.
A sundog. Half a sundog.

1, 2, 3, 4 ... turn.
I only saw it on the east-facing lap.
I looked for you there, Tom –
in the surprise, above the pierced light.
I convinced myself that if
I kept my eyes on the prize,
you would be there.
Reason and fantasy grappled and clung to each other
like exhausted boxers.
You were there; don't be silly, of course you aren't.
But maybe, maybe
this is a visitation.

The day after my brother was cremated
we waited in a small corridor at the base of an escalator
at LAX,
my daughter sat against the wall with her smartphone,

my husband pacing between the baggage carousel and
the corridor.
Finally a pair of loafers and tan trousers, a blue blazer
(dressed to fly) and my mother in black and red. Both solid,
grief pooling around their ankles, slowing their walk.
Mom looks to be 90 years old, shaking like a leaf.
I take her hand;
the tremor doesn't ease.

The day after my brother was cremated
slowly we began to gather.
From Dallas, Omaha, Minocqua, Moline,
from San Mateo, Miami, England and Chicago,
gathered in raven robes, vigilant for flashes
of colour and light,
clinging to life.

Here is the thing. At this moment, there is no empty space
where my generous, funny, opinionated brother was. My
head is full of him, as it never has been in all his 53 years.
I've dreamt of him as a child. Flashes of our intersecting
story fill my waking moments. He is closer to me now than
he ever was. And I don't particularly want to let go of this
time. I am surrounded by the people I know and love best
in the world (except for the sister stuck in Florida with an
ailing husband). I do not welcome the unravelling, the return
to busy distraction that drives all of my days.

***

The day after my brother was cremated
is over – it ended 4 hours ago.
In the three nights we've been in LA
I've awakened at 3am
and tried to occupy my mind with trivia.

Today though is Sunday, the day we will gather in a huge
Seventh Day Adventist church to remember, give thanks
and start to let the great unravelling begin. I am sat on
the bathroom floor of our hotel room, the extractor fan

competing with my thoughts for my attention, my back
up against the bathtub and my bottom on the floor, both
protected from the chill of tile by towels. And I am writing
about the sundog and the escalator and how Tom is filling
my head, Tom who I loved and scorned, who I most look
like in the family, who was my main competition for my
parents' affection and who usually won. Tom who could
slice me open with two words or a look. Tom whose
vulnerability mirrored mine and whose love I envied and
sought. He *was* a sundog, worshipped by my parents,
dazzling in light and colour, beloved as a pup ... fleeting,
incontrovertible, I keep my mind's eye on the sky. I cling to
the visitation, piercing to the heart, surprising, carried on
cirrus wisps. I return to the pool.

1, 2, 3, 4 ... turn.
The water is warm enough,
each exposed arm cuts
through the chill of the early morning air.
Slowly the sun moves up the rungs
of the urban pine,
my mind's eye sees the sundog
move higher and higher.

I complete my 25 laps of backstroke and float suspended.
I can watch no more.
I turn over,
swim a few strokes of front crawl to the steps
and submit my whole body to the chill,
the biting chill,
of a new day.

The day after my brother's memorial service

The day after my brother's memorial service
my father began to talk about Tom
    ('he had everything to look forward to')
and about resuming life
    ('on Saturday I'd like to have supper with the pastor;
    I'd like to have lunch with the Spellmeyers this week').

The day after my brother's memorial service
I realized:
> There is no consolation;
> there is only survival.
And I was strangely comforted by the thought.

The day after …
We accompanied my parents
> (so frail now)
> on a slightly complicated plane journey,
> carrying luggage they refused to check,
> arranging in-airport transport,
holding hands, offering an arm.

The day after …
Our bodies experienced a temperature change –
> 82 degrees Fahrenheit in five hours.
> An icy blast through the terminal door in Minneapolis.

The day after …
I slept eight full hours,
having not awakened at 3am for the first time
in the two weeks since the phone rang at that hour.
I awoke refreshed,
having had a dream about
choosing to take responsibility for my life energies and choices.

The day after …
is now over.
> I will carry the wound.
> Sometimes it will bleed.
> I will honour it
>> in my being
>> in my loving
>> in my living.

I will remember the knife cut of seeing his picture as we
entered the church, the slow desensitization of the photo
collage loop playing at the front of the church, the pain
unrelenting until pleasure erupted in knowing laughter
(This is our Tom), the energizing picture of Tom as a man
that connected to what I knew of him as a child – his life
coming into focus:
> his unique gift for friendship,
> his demand for connection,
> his playful, rascally sense of humour and rapier wit,
> his devotion to his family,
> the surprising breadth of his interests
> and high achievement as a surgeon
> despite 1000 rounds of golf in eight years.

Knowing him now, in the fullness of time, as I never knew
him before, a satisfaction.

Each day we drove the 2 Glendale Freeway from Burbank to
La Cañada-Flintridge, his route home from work; the road
he died on, marked with circling skids.

Each day I sat on his back garden platform ('Tom's Office')
in the sun, looking out towards hill and sky, marvelling
at trees once full of lemons and avocados, a few tenacious
fruits clinging to life in January.

Each day I relished in the affection of family, the hugs of
nieces, the tenderness of sister and sister-in-law, and other
connections woven by love and grief with Tom's friends.

Life is open and full, raw and abundant, in the midst
of death. The Real shatters defences and sweeps away
falsehood to reveal the golden cord and its quiet bindings.

I hate this event with all my heart, and I also cherish it.

My eyes are open.

Organ Failure

Thirteen days before you died,
you and Mom called
to sing me *Happy Birthday*.
The answerphone caught it.
Something in me couldn't erase
the message.

For weeks I had been aching
to cross the ocean to see you.
You were dismissive:
Don't spend the money!
I had just decided that,
in our regular Sunday evening call,
I would tell you that a post-Christmas visit
would be our Christmas gift.

Hours before I would make that call
I received the one alerting me to
sepsis and multiple organ failure.

Multiple organ failure.

There were times when I lamented the failure of your heart,
its laboured beating buttressed by a pacemaker-defibrillator
the size of a pack of playing cards implanted in your chest.
The heart that outlasted medical prognosis
by more than a decade.
A heart soft and enlarged
and resistant to regulation,
a heart out of control.

This is difficult to say and true:
Oft I lamented what felt to be
the failure of your heart
when thoughtless words burned
from your mouth to my heart.
No one else could cause
such searing pain.

I needed your approval

as much as oxygen
for most of my life.
And sometimes I received it.

But the taint of Eve,
my female contagion,
blinded you, would have perplexed you
if you had tried to understand,
if the straitjacket of gender chafed you
as it did me. Instead you wore it comfortably,
and assumed the fault was in me.

When I saw your lifeless body,
cold and devoid of defence,
I told you how much you pissed me off,
words tumbling out of my mouth,
words so truthful.
I said 'and I'm sure I pissed you off'.
The mutual discomfort
inherent in our very being,
part and parcel of our complicated love.

How I wanted to be known
and loved by you.

I was.
I know that now.
I have known it for years,
how love and longing
were a golden cord
binding heart to heart.

The failures in our relationship
were not failures of the heart
but failures of a different sort:
the failure to control a quick temper,
the failure to think before speaking,
the failure to enter each other's world.

Failures on both sides.
Generational failures.
Human condition failures.

Things my father gave to me

A capacity for hard work
Opinions held firmly
   sometimes too firmly
   for my own good and
   for anyone else's

A soft heart
A generous hand
A quick temper
A sharp tongue

Love of God
Hunger for knowledge
Searching wisdom

Complexity
Depth
Love

My mother
My sisters
My brother
Myself

Weather Talk (for my father)

Wading in the shallows,
feeling for the depths.

Long distance phone calls
majoring on the weather,
at the time frustrating,
wanting more,

now apparent as a deep expression
of love and connection.
Intimacy in the knowing receiving.

It was more than enough,
completed by mutual understanding.

The most beautiful thing

28 June 2015, 4:06am CST Wisconsin.

It was a blessing in the end.
Such is the gift of cancer –
death becomes a friend.

Now six hours later
I sit in her and Dad's pew
in the little Presbyterian church
that has been their home
for many years,
a pew I shared with them often,
holding Mom's hand briefly,
basking in Dad's glancing
scratch of my shoulder,
aware that my time
in this pew with them
was sacred and time-limited.

One of my earliest and strongest memories of my mother
is sitting next to her in our pew
on a Sunday in another small town church
more than fifty years ago.
The memory is of looking up at her profile
and thinking that she was
the most beautiful thing
in the whole wide world.

Often that memory has surfaced
these last weeks, as I became
more familiar with her body,
inside and out, than at any time bar
birth when we two were one.
I saw beauty in her well-lined face
and in our shared jowls.
Saw it in the length
between her nose and lips

and the parchment skin of her hands
delicate and veined.
I saw beauty in the fragility
of her shrinking shoulders,
her tiny frame increasingly apparent
beneath the protection of excess padding,
the waist I hadn't seen in years.
Saw it in her thick thighs and pretty feet,
the pixelated skin of her ankles and shins.

Through the weeks I saw beauty
in her enduring friendships and
the love of family which wove around us
a safety net for the high wire act
that is death.
I saw beauty in her acceptance
of the real and her bounding
of the possible.

I saw tendrils of beauty
in her reaching out
towards a lost daughter,
in her persevering conviction
that sisters should be friends
to one another,
in her joy at our being together.

My beautiful, beautiful mother.

There is the eternal in beauty
that never fades.
The dignity with which she faced her unexpected,
unfair and vanquishing illness will be manifest,
I pray, as I face adversity.
Her contentment, courage and compassion shall,
I believe, become compass points
in my choosing.
Her beautiful, aging, dying body,
I hope, will be the vehicle
for my acceptance of the fulfilment of my own.

Last Rites

It is hard to be present to the lastness of things.
We have the experience, but can't fathom the meaning
   until time has passed. (T. S. Eliot)

'This is my last day in my house,' she said
the morning the hospice ambulance was scheduled to come.

Often we do not know it is the last time.
Often we do not want to know.

This Sunday, a week after her death,
is the last time I will worship with these people.
I know it, though I do not want to.

The vintage choir and determined organist,
the quirky 'Amen and Amen'
and other habits of the congregation,
the stories half-glimpsed, mostly untold,
that each one brings.
The memory of my father's joy as liturgist,
my mother's caring calm, and now
the embrace of long-time friends
who seek to ease our pain and their own
in the deaths of my parents.

There is lastness, and there is lasting.
My mind turns towards the lasting in human experience:
the earnest endeavour of entreating the Beyond,
the striving and struggling of trembling flesh,
the holiness of tears, the assurance of touch.
These shall be forever
so long as flesh inhabits the earth.

This is the last time, here and now, with this and these.

Buried deep within
the lastness of this time
is the lasting:
the endurance of love,

the cherishing of memory,
the kindness of near-strangers,
the hope that drives us to gather
and encourages us to disperse
to bless the world
and all that is in it.

God bless all of our last times,
　　known and unknown,
and lift us
at the last
into the love
that lasts
forever.

Death's undoing

Scrambling to pick up pieces,
to patch together enough
life and warmth.

Death's undoing becomes
the great reweaving,
tattered bits pulled through
　　warp and weft
shimmer under a tender gaze.

It is a labour of love …
the pulling of threads,
the weaving of memories,
the patient contemplation
　　that sees beauty amidst brokenness,
the great thanksgiving.

Grief's Pool

I swim around the edge
of the dark pool,
obsidian overflow of grief,
contained yet brimming,
a thing of fearsome beauty,
magnetic.

I still myself, willing
to go with the current.
Slowly circling arms
and a slight kick
keep me afloat.
It is necessary
to conserve energy.

I dip below the surface,
and bob up,
clear water
streaming from my face,
run my hands
over my head.

I contemplate
full descent.
It is not my time.

I turn and float,
face to the sky,
letting the elements
hold me up,
cradle me as once
my parents cradled
their firstborn.

Suspended in time,
I whisper their names.

For my mother

You held my hand lightly
in this pew,
not for too long,
your smile warm,
your eyes glistening.

I knew then
that the time would come
when you would not be
here
to hold my hand.

But I did not know
how painful your going
would be

or how present your love
would remain,

or how that light touch
would prepare me

to receive
gratefully
whatever is given.

To receive it,
a gift of grace.

Stardust

1.

Light years before you were born,
deep within a giant cloud of dust and gas
at an unimaginably cold temperature,
atoms started to bind and, collapsing
under their own gravity, accreted mass
that in time –
   a very long time –
        became stars.

I've travelled thousands of miles
to bring you to this hospital.
Just as winter ended, the spring light
clean and cool, you called with the news:
stage 4 metastasized melanoma,
that in time –
   a very short time –
        will take you to dust.

You were light to me. Your smile the first
I laid my infant eyes on. The soft skin
of your arms my nursery. Your cooing my
first song. Your approval my delight.

And then you were not. I needed other light,
and I needed to learn my own shining.
I left the nursery and wandered a wide world.
You kept my place at the table.

I help you onto another table. Your legs,
resolutely earthbound, do not want to go.
I slip off your slip-on shoes and take
your glasses. Your purse is on my shoulder.

The room is cold. I feel as though I will
collapse under the weight of this gravity.

2.

The kindly technician invites me to join her
on the other side of a windowed wall,
where we watch the magnetic tube move
up and down your body, mapping ...

The screen on her desk thrums and I see
hundreds of moving pinpricks of light
against a dark sky. Slowly they are drawn
towards each other, collapsing
under the weight of their own gravity,
accreting mass until they become
your skeleton, whole and intact.

The wonder of it has not left me.

3.

Weeks after the bone scan,
   weeks of tenderness and tears,
you returned full bore to the dark sky.

There,
shining brightly,
defiant amidst the dust,
you will give yourself, in time –
   a very long time –
       to life again.

On the Road

The Storm

Out of nowhere
it blew in, all rage,
wind-whipped water
beating the windows,
shaking the trees.

Roots grip earth more firmly.
I release my grip.

I draw back the blinds
to witness the power,
grateful for storm,
   mirror of my soul,
and for shelter.

Fissures have been fissing.
I heard the rumbling,
dutifully reported it,
but was unprepared
when the earth cracked
and I fell in
to the weeping and wailing
waves of grief and pain,
a suspicion of failure
subdued:
This is.

It can be no other way.
We are who, how we are.

I will ride this storm
until it casts me out
on some far shore
which will be Home.

Go to your cell

'It will teach you everything.'

Here I hide,
free from
the demands
of others,
if I dare.

Here I am,
free to
feel the band
tightening
around my chest,
not knowing
if it is
friend,
foe,
or both.

Here I am,
free from
the nibbles
of dozens of mouths
that seek to
eat my flesh,
tear my heart,
gobble my brains,
as if that would
give them
life, heedless
that they are taking
mine away.

Here I hide,
free to see
that their need
gave me

purpose, gave me
a tune to whistle
while I worked,
muffling the song
my soul most
wants (and fears)
to sing.

(So close to that song
is the whistling tune,
so satisfying is the work,
that my soul was glad
to hide in the deep,
dark recesses,
biding its time,
listening
to the heartbeat
of life itself.)

Today I awake
to birdsong,
regular, relentless,
and wonder:
am I
strong
enough, courageous
enough
to risk
singing.
To step
away
from the yearning
of others' hearts
to listen
to mine.

I clear
my throat.

The Vow

As tears are silent,
so too would I be.

Each escaped sigh
seeking Source.

As clouds are silent,
so too would I be.

My presence a wisp,
my holding a promise:

> shade from searing heat,
> water for parched land.

As trees are silent,
so too would I be.

The rustling of my leaves
the signature of the wind.

As ice is silent,
so too would I be.

In silvered puddle
or sugar-crusted lawn:

> the time of fallow
> a sheltering grace.

Sea Wind

Sea wind,
wild and strong,
blow through
the misconceptions
that cloud
my sight.

Sharp hail,
angular, crisp,
sting my skin
like Isaiah's coal,
cleansing,
enlivening.

Crashing waves,
relentless and rhythmic,
turn the stone
of my heart
to sand
and salve.

Broad horizon,
sea-lined and -crested,
call me forth
into the new day,
transfigured
by hope.

January 2015, Northumbria Community

Blood Donation

For years I was a faithful blood donor,
the kind that disdained
the failure of others to give.
I even convinced (by example)
my husband to take up the habit.

Then my brother was killed,
and the giving impulse in me
began to dry up.

I stopped.

It is fourteen months later.
I am as unwilling as ever,
maybe more so.

The deficit has only grown;
parts of my heart have become a vast desert.
The wind whips up sandstorms and shifts terrain,
exposing ancient ruins and empty reservoirs,
and I watch, eyes stung from flung sand,
vision strained and searching.

The invitation to sacrifice,
to 'lose my life to save it',
causes me to slam shut
the Good Book.

My heart is
no stone;
it needs
all the blood
it can muster
for the task
of choosing
life.

Mark 8.31–38

What if?

What if my resistance
and my fear,
my closing up
   in the face of need
   and unwanted expectation
is You – pulling
on the cord
that binds me to You,
saying:

Come to me,
   rest,
   heal,
   be

– and let your beautiful
self be
renewed and reshaped
for the healing of the world?

Breathe

Beneath my shattered sadness
a silent joy begins to grow,
a coming home
to who I am.

It slips between my fingers

It slips between my fingers
   this faith that once sustained me.
The graceful cup I make with my hands
prefers emptiness now,
   the kiss of wind,
     the memory of water.

I let go, of what?
Not joy or simplicity.
Not the power of silence
   or of paying attention.
Not friendship.
Not poetry.
Not love.
Never love.

Before the ground around me
   becomes quicksand,
I quietly slip away,
   not wishing to disturb others,
   just wanting to make space,
to feel
my way
to solid ground.
A place I can stand with ease,
and dance and laugh
and cry and rest.

Long ago I shed one skin.
Now I begin to shed another.

Earthing

All that is needful has been provided.
And here's me –
   roots dangling in thin air,
   straining towards water,
   yearning for warm soil,
     hungry,
        thirsty.

I am looking for what
will feed parts of me that have been starved,
will anchor me in high winds,
will spark my flowering.

I am not satisfied

I am not satisfied
   with the tongue-tripping platitude
   the quick response
   the assured answer.

Better to walk in the dark
with a willing heart
and a flickering flame
than to flip an electric switch
meant to assuage anxiety
and dispel shadow.

I will only be satisfied
   with the complex Real
   with the challenge of owning failure
     and maintaining hope
   with the courage called forth
that forges the new day.

On the road

The road is littered
with discarded remnants,
garments that no longer fit,
ideas found unsuitable
for real life:
tiaras,
torn hairshirts,
split-soled shoes.

Today I arise,
paw through a closet
reflecting a life's work
of identity accumulation,
past the clergy shirts
and smart suits,
and choose a stylishly plain
grey dress with pockets
and flat shoes I can walk in.

I will preach in this garb,
no robe, no collar,
only the clothes
that cover my nakedness
that I may seek
to reveal our humanity
and our striving
to touch holiness.

Innumerable small deaths
prepare the way
for life.

Kintsugi (Gathering the Fragments)

In the seventh decade of my life,
I begin to gather the fragments.
White gloves on my hands,
I reach for each shard,
hold it to the light,
feel the sharp edges
and polished surfaces,
say a prayer. *So be it.*

Innocence a memory;
illusion shattered.
The floor is littered
with tattered fabric
(the veil rent)
and shimmering insight
awaiting harvest.

The Real has broken through.
The mirror smashed
shows more truth
then ever the whole
intact could.

The best laid plans
were founded
on unstable ground,
over land liable to sinkholes
and vulnerable to seismic shifts.

Leaps of hope
were more costly
than ever imagined.

Death has come
as warning and friend,
wise counsel
and clarion
call.

Pure attention,
the soul awake,
is exposed as the
alchemical element
that unleashes
possibility
and channels
love.

Slowly the fragments
reassemble,
gold filaments binding
disparate pieces,
a harvest of beauty,
a container for
life.

Beginner's Mind

And now
nearly 30 years after
my first faltering *Yes*,
I come again to
sacred space
cradled in eternity,
hallowed by prayer.

Fabric permeated by incense
holds tremulous chant,
ancient words reach
towards the elegant
arch of the ceiling
mirroring the silent
arc of the universe.

Years of loss and
confusion fall away;
even the offence of patriarchy
subsides, to reveal the wonder of
a whole enough soul
able to stand undefended
before the Holy.

Beginner's mind
welcomes the moment
to stand at the fulcrum
of eternity, blessing yesterday
and opening to tomorrow.

Mirfield, Trinity Sunday

Redemption Road

I stepped forward
as only I could,
not knowing.

Not knowing
and limping, only certain
of what I could no longer do,
of who I no longer was.

Not looking
this way or that; not wanting
much. Some safety,
time and space
to breathe.

Grace can't help herself.
She sees an empty space
and pushes in. She feels
a bleeding heart and
intuits the balm. She knows
the way the body needs to walk.

Slowly the miracles accrete –
undesired invitations
open new vistas, chance
conversations seed fruitful
friendships, nudges lead
to surprising reconciliations, slowly
the heart begins to heal.

And what I have done and could do,
who I have been and will be, become
of a piece, of a peace.

Vocation Prayer

Help me to hold lightly
to my minor attractions,
dislikes and disaffections,
that I may hear clarion
the song of my soul
and see the Way
unfold before me.

Endurance

Endurance of necessity
requires flexibility.

The tree that endures
will bend in the wind,
 its leaves aflutter.

Even old trees have
enough give to survive.

A lifetime of being buffeted
 builds resilience,
  strengthens the core,
   drives roots deep in the earth.

Sunday morning

I will walk to church today,
take the sanctuary
within me outside
to meet the sanctuary
of earth and sky.

I will walk to church today,
let the rhythm of my feet
match the beat of my heart
tuned to the beat of the Great
Heart that gave me life.

I will walk to church today,
eyes awake to wonder awaiting,
ears open to the praise songs
of birds and beetles
shaking off winter's sloth.

I will walk to church today,
shaking off my own sloth,
preparing to meet my Maker
and my making, in bread
and wine, in word and silence.

I will walk to church today.

The Sea

Strange comfort, this.

A bracing wind,
   the roll of waves,
      a slate grey sky.

The eternal sea
   – birth and death,
   eating and being eaten –
relentlessly scours stones
   and shifts sand.

Here,
   in storm or calm,
peace descends.
The eye,
   drawn to an endless horizon,
drinks it in.
The heart,
   the longing heart,
slows to time and tide.

A hand opens, softly.
A sigh escapes barely parted lips.

To know oneself,
   a tiny grain of sand
      on an immense shore
before the ceaseless sea.

Grace is grace. It comes.[1]

Sat on the hard bench
in a snug black cassock
in the prayer place,
Love is written anew on my heart.

My heart is macerated in Love:
Love writ on the outside,
Love soaking into the fibres, the fissures, the fractures.
Love seeking the smallest hiding places;
Love emblazoned, encrypted, encapsulating.

I pray that each heartbreak to come will
crack the stone
and allow more Love to seep in.

I pray that my first desire will be
understanding,
not judgement.

I pray that my last breath will be
a long exhalation of Love,
its molecules infecting the air.

I pray that I will not forget this moment
when grace again reclaimed a heart
bruised and battered and bereft.

I pray.

---

[1] Jones, Serene, 2009, *Trauma and Grace*, Louisville KY: Westminster Press, p. 73.

Walking with Sophia

Wisdom walks in silence,
in wonder to behold
the greening leaf and purple flower
proclaiming June so bold.

Wisdom walks in chatter:
the birds are on the wing.
While wild geese honk encouragement
the skylarks start to sing.

Wisdom walks awake, aware,
she doesn't miss a thing:
she knows the way the wind blows,
she dodges nettles' sting.

Wisdom breathes and wisdom sighs,
her purview over all
gives her unbounded pleasure,
sharpens her sense of call.

Wisdom pleads and wisdom cries,
Wake up! The time is here!
The day grows short, the hour is come,
what you must do is clear.

Wisdom weeps and wisdom groans,
whilst we prepare for war
and close our borders, shrink our hearts
and fear the distant shore.

Wisdom creeps into our dreams,
she waits outside our door.
She won't relent, she won't give up
until we beg for more.

Wisdom walks intrepidly
on paths the saints have trod.
And where she steps wild flowers bloom
within the mind of God.

On St Hilda's Way, North York Moors

Coming Home

How lovely to become
an old woman.
To sit and watch, unnoticed,
the rush and passion
of life's striving for itself.

How lovely to sit
in a comfortable chair
with a cup of peppermint tea,
and nothing to do
but write this poem.

Death has become
an acquaintance.
Dreams and visions
broader, bolder, freer;
colours richer, softer.

Puddles are aflame
on a sodden trail
as the sun sets
and I walk
towards Home.

Now

She holds joy
   a shining yellow globe
her touch light,
her arms fluid
   and astonished.

Words become roses
   blooming outwards
from a still centre.

Angels hover
   to catch the scent
and smile.

Meditation on the painting Tarn Beck Falls in Winter Spate *(painter: Carla McGowan)*

She has become the river,
her breasts floating and solid
as water swirls around them.

Her legs tributaries
of glacial freshness.

Her arms stretched
to embrace forests.

Her torso, fluid, dances.
Golden gorse applauds.

In rushing movement,
she renews the face of the earth.

In wonder

I pitch my tent in wonder.
Roiling clouds
kiss mountains.
Electric green
carpets the hillside.

New Psalms and Prayers

Psalm for the Newly Born

Fresh as dew,
made of stardust and dreams,
tender touch and deepest longing,
we welcome you.

Your fingernails the memory of ocean beds.
The furrow of your brow the future of the race.
Your hand's grasp around my finger a sacrament.

Called forth by love,
you call forth our own.
Every mother's breast swells;
every father's legs brace.
A fierce tenderness arises
to protect you in every storm
and guard you against every fear.
The gratitude of grandparents
beholds you in wonder.

Child of our plenty,
we pray for you
freedom from want.
Daughter of courage,
we summon for you
the strength to meet
every challenge.
Son of costly love,
we dream a world at peace
and pledge our troth
to God's new day.

Written for Jane Okee Youngblood
July 2014

Psalm for the Seed

In the beginning
   the scattering of seed
   the desire to spread joy
   the love that overflows

A word falls into fertile ground –
   the shelter and structure of soil
(all that has happened)
     a nourishing bed,
   the dark damp
     a cocooning grace.

Within the word a seed
   that grows towards light,
     never before its time.

The dark nurtures a fragile hope,
in hiddenness
     life takes shape
     sense is made
     strength gathered
in the place of unknowing
below the surface
in the silent hall
where the Holy bids us
tarry.

Under the gaze of God we grow
     limbs stretch and flex
     vision clarifies
     new words take shape
horizons broaden
possibilities emerge.

Published for Rural Mission Sunday 2016, available at www.germinate.net; reprinted with kind permission.

Harvest Psalm

Sing of the miracle:
a harvest so joyful.
Where barren land once stretched
upon our mem'ries etched,
a field of green and gold,
a wonder to behold.

Sing of the miracle:
a sheltering home.
The smallest of seeds
yields meeting of needs:
dwelling for sparrow,
and shade for the morrow.

Sing of the miracle:
a myst'ry we feast on.
Of sowing and sleeping,
of growth set for reaping,
of strong backs a-scything,
and crops fit for tithing.

Sing of the miracle:
the goodness of God.
Whose generous sowing
begets our great growing,
beyond our scant knowing,
with grace overflowing.

Woodland Wedding Psalm

We call upon these persons here present ...

Cathedral of earth and sky
and all that is within and beyond,
you are witnesses
to the ancient story
made fresh in the love
that has made this day.

Tallest tree and smallest flower,
fed by the sun's kiss,
strengthened by the wind's caress,
attend this miracle.
Watch over the lovers
who pledge their troth.
Shelter their dreams;
draw their delight.
Let no harm come.

Stones, provide steps;
Let stumbling be met
with a hand up.
Fallen logs,
welcome rest;
Let weariness be met
with kindness.

You, blackbird, hear the song
whose breath gives life,
and squirrel, see the treasure
unearthed that sees us
through the winter
of our lives.
Earthworms, wriggle
to nourish the seeds
that push through
dark and damp
to light and life.

Red fox, stop to smell
the freshness
of this moment, the aroma
of birth and death, of bodies
joined in hope and hallowing,
of hands entwined
forevermore
to grasp the gift
and drink the cup
together.

Friends gathered,
taste the sweetness
of longing fulfilled,
risk taken,
tenderness shared.

There is no greater triumph,
no stronger power,
no thing more wondrous
than this:
that these two
love each other
with body and mind,
soul and might.

Praise be to the Love
that makes it so;
world without end,
Amen.

For Cara and Carolyn, July 2015

Psalm for the Dead

First, the sound with no name,
the terrible wrench
that starts in the bowels, the groin, the womb,
and roars up, collecting agony,
before, erupting,
it pierces the room.

Then the silence, long and hard,
the gathering gloom,
the harvesting of fragments,
a scouring memory
invaded by the presence
of the one who will not be seen
except in dreams
and worn photographs
with tattered edges.

An undertow of grief
greys the day.
An overflow of weariness
greets the night.
Dullness offers
a saving detachment.

Beneath the surface,
all is being rearranged.
Every truth,
all assumptions,
the very foundations
are torn asunder and await
a patient reordering,
the graced reweaving
that will permit
a different kind of living,

the hard won knowledge
of life's fragility,
death's corporeal finality
and, in time,
   a long time,
Love's eternity.

Psalm of Praise

Fulfil the law: Praise!

Lift your face to the sun,
listen to the song of birds
and the sigh of the wind.

Breathe deeply.
Lend a hand to those in need;
lay down at night in gratitude.

Sing and dance as joy moves you.
Weep when you are aggrieved.
Bring your best to the task ahead.

Live with kindness.
Pray with expectation.

Commend one another
to God who made us
and loves all that She creates.

Psalm of Lament

Holy One, keeper of the days
    and keeper of my tears,
I turned to you in hope.
I used my best skills,
    my energy and my passion
    to lead your people,
but then came the fall,
the unintended consequence,

with little warning.

I fell into the pain
and it became my own.
Deep was the pit.
I was consumed;
there was no way out.

And yet – you tenderly led me
from the shadows into the light.

You bathed my wounds with compassion.
You revealed to me my weakness,
    and gave me courage to stand
    on ground I could trust.
You gave me silence
so that my words could do no harm.
You held me as I rejected old ideas
and stretched to embrace the new.

I stand humbled
in grace and reverence
to offer, once more,
my praise.

Psalm of Rest

I rest in Thee
as flowers rest in earth,
drawing nourishment
from life in death.

I rest in Thee
as earth rests on clay,
assured foundation,
structure that permits form.

I rest in Thee
as ocean rests on seabed,
trusting sand to contain
the wild dance of waves.

I rest in Thee
as whales rest in ocean,
singing their gratitude,
sounding their friendship.

I rest in Thee.

Ode to Courage

Praise the souls with sight undimmed
who – seeing wrong – seek right to make
who – seeing void – step up to create.

Praise the fire of anger,
and praise the firm resolve.

Praise the gilded tongue, the stirring speech, the rallying cry.
Praise the refusal to be seduced
  by words that speak of life but deal in death.
Praise the powerful pen, the unyielding vision, the
  earnest prayer.
Praise the poem. Praise the bankrolling cheque.

Praise the trouble-makers, the risk-takers, the time-shapers.

Praise the resilient, long road walkers;
Praise quiet voices, whispering hope.

Praise each manifestation of courage that graces the planet,
each gaze that lifts towards the horizon,
each step that protests impoverishment,
each word and each silence that speaks hope.

Praise erect posture, steely gaze, unapologetic being.
Praise refusal to bow, assertion of place, resolute articulation.

Praise power grabbed and grasped and wielded with skill
in the face of all that diminishes and degrades.

Praise pissed off women and bolshie Black people,
and people in wheelchairs who block the entrance because
  they can't get in.
Praise gay folk who refuse the closet and transwomen with
  facial hair.

Praise life, praise life, praise life.

Prayer for Awakening I

The beautiful impulse
   – the dignity of the person,
   freedom of conscience –
that gives birth to nations,

So powerful,
so painfully marred
by the elevation of crude,
unthinking selfishness
and greed.

I weep for this land,
for the many
who now
   (again and more so)
live in fear
and desperation.

God, raise us up
to claim and to share
the vision
that gives us life.

Prayer for Awakening II

There are consequences
to our conveniences.

May we move slowly through life,
discerning thoughtfully,
choosing wisely,

that we might account for our actions
to the seventh generation.

Prayer for the start of a new week

Give to me patience
to complete the tasks ahead,
power to shape my work
with a blessing hand,
and peace to lay aside
that which must wait.

Grace me with acceptance of my limits,
and wisdom in my choosing
what to pick up and what to set down.

Grant to me the generosity
to invite others into
the creativity and joy of your life.

Prayer of Thanksgiving for Enduring Love

It is the first commandment, and the last.
As Jesus sat for the last time among those he loved most,
he said: *Abide in my love;*
love one another.

We needed to be reminded.
For, day by day, we find love difficult.
Sometimes it is the distraction
of things to do, tasks to accomplish, work to finish.
But, as often, it is a matter of short-sighted selfishness;
our own needs and desires take centre stage.

To give oneself to love,
over a long period of time,
is an act of courage and an act of hope:
Courage to face oneself,
in the daily effort of remembering
that the world does not revolve around me,
and of making sacrifices of time and energy
directed toward the other; and
Hope that we will find ourselves
accepted and loved as we are,
as we forgive and are forgiven
our frailties and failures.

In this crucible of giving and receiving, wounding and
    forgiving,
we are formed in the image in which we were made.
We were made by Love, in love and for love.
Its patient exercise will reveal our hidden depths and
    capacities.
In truth, we are for each other.

And so we pray:
God, grant us the grace to endure in our loving day by day,
that you might be made manifest in our flesh,
and we might find our joy complete. Amen.

John 15.9–12

Mother's Day Prayer

God, make me vigorous in giving birth,
in bearing child.
Make me strong and wise and crafty and resilient.
Make my breath deep and nourishing,
my hands strong and sure.
See how this dust,
wet by tears and formed by loving hands,
becomes pliable and durable.
See the beauty of the form which
holds the treasure and shares it out.

God, make me courageous in facing death,
in letting go.
Make me gentle and kind and forgiving and vulnerable.
Make my words sound and true,
my being calm and spacious.
See how this fear,
wrenching my gut,
becomes my strength.
See how this brokenness
opens the way to wholeness.

Strong Prayer

I will pray this way.

I will stand tall, back straight,
core engaged, legs strong;
my arms open in W-form –
   opening my ribcage,
   my heart, my lungs;
   my palms to the sky.

My face tilted up,
   neck exposed.
My breath even,
   deep, nourishing.

Only my eyelids are closed,
that I may totally inhabit myself
without distraction.

Meet me, O God.

Meet my strength
and make it yours.

Divine Sex

Inhale my tongue,
   That your exhale may breathe life into weary limbs,
   That my mouth may birth new words.

Invite my caress,
   That my skin may call forth strength and tenderness,
   That my hands may grow sure.

Ignite my passion,
   That you may discover your incompleteness without me,
   That our union may bear fruit.

Embodied Ministry Conference, 2014

Song for Petticoe Wick

My mother the sea.

Her salty, fluid being
envelops me
as I power through the swells,
among iridescent sea gooseberries
  – tiny blimps
  of shimmering translucence –
over beds of waving kelp
sheltering small fish.

Here, strength
becomes glide
becomes a return
to beginnings.

The primordial broth; genesis.
All of life holds
the ancient memory.

Lifting my head, the squawk
of cliff-nesting seabirds
fills my ears; the stink
of guano-crusted rock my nose.
Swell and squawk,
stink and shimmer,
my mother the sea surprises;
less nursery, more wild ride.

I turn onto my back,
face the blue sky,
catch the sun's warmth,
then flip again.

My stroke lengthens,
I am coming home,
    coming home,
        coming home.

O bright joy!

The Way of St Cuthbert – poems and prayers

A prayer for beginning a journey

[Day one, Melrose to Maxton 11 miles]

Pry open this cynical heart
Peel away the defences
   that accrete day by day
Make way for wonder
as footsteps become
metres, become miles,
and the wind strips away
the unnecessaries that cloud
vision and weigh footfall.

Make mountains become
molehills and worries become
windows and me become
we.

Make tired become
strength and terrain become
pathway and foe become
friend.

Make quiet become joy,
make chatter become birdsong
make earth become home.

Prayer for a long day

[Day two, Maxton to Cessford 13.5 miles]

Unclench my jaw and my fists
and enable me to walk
with patience and appreciation
throughout the day.

Make laughter light.
Make song strong.
Make friendship possible.

Under a hot sun,
melt resistance
to what is unwelcome.

By a light breeze,
cool frayed tempers
and defuse frustration.

Before a heartening vista,
give a vision
of a whole community
walking as one
within your merciful embrace.

Prayer for ascent

[Day three, Cessford to Kirk Yetholm 9.5 miles]

Receive the full weight of my being
Read the tilt of my body as a leaning into you
Render my soul to be fit for heaven on earth

Steady my walk
Surprise my eyes
Sync my heart
   With the rhythms of the Way

Bring us to the top
To witness your glory
And sing your praise.

A prayer to enter the wilderness

[Day four, Kirk Yetholm to Wooler 13.5 miles]

The wilderness beckons.

Meet us there
as you met our forebears,
mothers and fathers of the Way
who sought you amidst the crags,
on the high places,
their laboured steps rewarded
in still moments of wonder.

Meet us there,
on the path that holds
echoes of saints' footsteps,
where birdsong shatters silence
and the slightest breeze sets trees sighing,
where the heart's posture returns to its natural state
of bowed reverence and quiet gratitude.

Meet us there.
Show us the signs of others' sojourns,
the evidence of women and men long gone
who walked in these hills and left their mark,
who fought their battles and searched for sustenance,
who laid down at night, weary and worn,
whose deepest needs were no different than ours.

Meet us each place we wander.
Lift our eyes to new horizons,
Teach us new ways to praise.

Prayer among the Cheviots

[Day five, Wooler to Fenwick 11 miles]

(after day four)

Easter Tor
Black Law
Tom Tallon Crag
Yeavering Bell
Harehope Hill
Hart Heugh

The names
trip over the tongue,
tumble and cascade
as long ago molten earth
tumbled and cascaded
when continents
   – Avalonia, Laurentia –
collided, exploding volcanically
to form an otherworldly
upland of endless hills
folding over valleys:
College, Harthope,
Breamish, Bowmont,
Heatherhope.

Here an ancient crevasse,
ice-cracked rock
now smothered in green.

Bracken, fern and thistle,
crackly heather, angular stands
of trees saluting feather-clouded
blue skies sheltering
lapwing, curlew, grouse
   – Go back, go back, go back –
winged mamas distract to protect.

In foothills where ancient
people hauled heavy rocks
for sanctuary and defence,
long-horned goats
roam and scatter,
avoiding the infrequent
incursions of ramblers.

Chanted, the names
  – hills, valleys,
    flora, fauna –
become a litany of glory,
a gratitude to eternal forces,
the assurance,
the stark beauty,
of life beyond
our ken and control,
a paean of praise,
a whispered thank you.

A pilgrim prayer

[Day six, Fenwick to Holy Island 7 miles]

I glimpsed you from afar,
through mist and rain,
your strong walls standing
above silvered pools
of a withdrawing tide.

There, on Mons Gaudi,
my heart rejoiced
and my body was glad

to see the longed for
journey's end and heart's desire,
to see it and know it as Home.

I would walk
on my knees
these last miles;
each advance a prayer.

I would close my eyes
and navigate by inner sense,
as a swallow makes its way
north over the Sahara,
and a puffin south
from the Atlantic
to its North Sea nest.

I would let the song
of my soul guide me,
my deepest desire
mapping the way.

So the longing
for heaven on earth
guides us day by day.

So glimpses of kindness,
the best of who we can be,
shine a light on the path.

So the strong hands
and generous hearts
of companions make short,
make joyful, the journey.

A prayer for journey's end (a new beginning)

May the mud
that clings to my rucksack
and rings my toenails
beckon memories of
the silence of sand,
the song of seals and
the staves that point towards
the heart's destination.

May the ache
and the restlessness
of muscles become accustomed
to movement
keep me walking
the pilgrim Way
with patience
and perseverance.

May the sound of laughter
evoke the delight of discovery
and the pleasure of companions,
the possibilities of friendship.
May I not neglect the stranger,
within and outwith,
who may open new doors
to life and to love.

May the God of heaven and earth
keep us all,
now and forever,
Amen.

Scripture Index

Genesis 17.1–16	23–4	Mark 1.1–8	4–5
Genesis 21.1–21	39	Mark 1.4–11	13
Genesis 32.22–32	38	Mark 1.9–15	24
Exodus 2.1–10	25	Mark 1.12–13	21
Exodus 16.2–15	40	Mark 4.10–12	53
Exodus 19; 20	41	Mark 7.31–37	51
Exodus 20.1–17	26	Mark 8.31–38	90
Leviticus 19.1–2	19	Mark 9.2–9	20
Deuteronomy 34	42	Mark 10.46–52	52
1 Samuel 1.20–28	12	Mark 13.1–8	51
1 Kings 19	18	Luke 1.26–38	5
1 Kings 19.8–13a	43	Luke 1.39–45	9
2 Kings 2.1–12	44	Luke 2.33–35	12
Psalm 1	14	Luke 3.7–18	4–5
Isaiah 6.1–8	45	Luke 3.15–17, 21–22	13
Isaiah 40.1–11	4–5	Luke 8.9–10	53
Isaiah 45.1–7	44	Luke 10.38–42	53
Jeremiah 1.4–10	17	Luke 13.10–17	54
Jeremiah 8.4–9.1	46	Luke 15.1–10	55
Jeremiah 17.5–10	14	Luke 17.11–19	56
Amos 8	46	Luke 18.1–18	57
Habakkuk 2	47	Luke 18.9–14	55
		Luke 19.1–11	58
Matthew 1.18–25	6–8, 9	Luke 24.36–48	35
Matthew 2.1–12	13	John 2.13–22	26
Matthew 2.13–18	11	John 3.1–17	22
Matthew 3.13–17	13	John 11.1–45	28
Matthew 4	42	John 13.1–17, 31b–35	30
Matthew 4.12–25	1	John 14.23–29	37
Matthew 5.1–12	48	John 15.1–18	36
Matthew 5.21–37	16	John 15.9–12	119
Matthew 7.24–27	49	Romans 12.1–9	58
Matthew 15.10–28	39	1 Corinthians 1.18–31	27
Matthew 16.21–28	39	Philippians 4.4–9	57
Matthew 22.1–14	50	2 Thessalonians	
Matthew 26.17–20, 26–30	31	1.11–2.2	58